STRANGER THAN FICTION II

by MARTIN WALSH

SCHOLASTIC INC.
New York Toronto London Auckland Sydney

ISBN 0-590-41575-1

Copyright © 1978 by Martin Walsh. All rights reserved. Published by Scholastic Inc.

12 11 10 9 8 7 6 5 4 3   2/9

Printed in the U.S.A.   01

Contents

Can We See the Future?

Is it possible to foretell the future? Do all of us have within us the ability to sense events that will occur at some future date? Are some people more sensitive to premonitions of the future than others? What about the role of dreams in predicting the future?

These are difficult questions to answer and research in these areas is in its infancy. But many of the world's great events have been predicted beforehand. In our century no two historical events have been foreshadowed more than the assassination of President Kennedy in 1963 and the sinking of the *Titanic* in 1912. The predictions of impending doom before both of these events are uncanny in their accuracy.

President John F. Kennedy's assassination was foretold by many people. Jeanne Dixon, famous seer of Washington, D.C., predicted President Kennedy's assassination many years beforehand.

In 1952 Jeanne Dixon received a vision in which the White House suddenly appeared in radiant brilliance with the numerals 1960 formed above. In front of the White House stood a young man, tall and blue-eyed, with thick brown hair. An inner voice told her that he was a Democrat. Then a dark cloud spread over the numbers and an inner voice told Jeanne Dixon that the young man would meet with a violent death.

In the May 13, 1956, issue of *Parade Magazine*, still four years before President Kennedy's inauguration, reporters interviewed Mrs. Dixon concerning her predictions. The reporters were astounded when she said, "A blue-eyed Democratic president elected in 1960 will be assassinated."

The reporters, shocked by her words, suggested that they might say simply that he would "die in office."

"Say it as you like, but he will be assassinated," replied Mrs. Dixon.

Throughout John Kennedy's term as President, Jeanne Dixon continued seeing the dark cloud over the White House.

In the summer of 1963 the President's

three-day-old son, Patrick, died. Friends suggested that this may have caused the dark cloud.

"It cannot be," explained Mrs. Dixon, "because I still see a large coffin being carried into the White House. This means that the President will meet death elsewhere and his body will be returned there for national mourning."

Then in late November of 1963 Jeanne Dixon was attending a luncheon in the Presidential Dining Room of the Mayflower Hotel in Washington.

Mrs. Dixon appeared to be in a state of depression and was unable to eat. When asked why she wasn't eating Mrs. Dixon replied, "I just can't. I'm too upset. Something is going to happen to the President today . . ."

The luncheon continued. Then suddenly the music being played by Sidney Seidenman's orchestra ceased and the conductor came to the table where Mrs. Dixon was seated.

"Someone has just tried to take a shot at the President," said Seidenman.

."The President is dead," replied Mrs. Dixon sadly.

"No, no, he isn't. He may not even have been struck," insisted Seidenman.

"You will learn that he is dead," replied Mrs. Dixon in the same tone of voice.

Seidenman rushed from the room but returned quickly. "I heard it on the radio," he said. "He's still alive, and they're going to give him a blood transfusion."

"The radio is wrong." Mrs. Dixon said finally. "President Kennedy is dead. I tried to send a warning to him, but no one would listen. Now it's too late."

The date was November 22, 1963. Jeanne Dixon's prophecy had come true just as she said it would.

Stranger even than the death of Kennedy were the unbelievable predictions concerning the sinking of the *Titanic* in 1912.

In 1898, fourteen years before the sinking of the *Titanic*, author Morgan Robertson wrote a book which is uncanny in its similarities to the *Titanic*. Robertson's book, entitled *Futility*, told the story of a ship called, amazingly enough, the *Titan*. The *Titan* carried 3,000 passengers compared with 2,207 for the *Titanic*. The *Titan* could reach a maximum speed of 25 knots compared with 23 knots for the *Titanic*. The Titan had 24 lifeboats, the *Titanic*, 20. The *Titan* was 800 ft. long and had a displacement of 75,000 tons. The *Titanic* was 882.5 ft. long with a displacement of 66,000 tons. Each ship also had three propellors.

These statistics are remarkable in their similarities, but the comparisons don't end there. The *Titan* was called "unsinkable" because of its special construction. The *Titanic* was also thought to be unsinkable, but both ships sunk after colliding with icebergs. Amazingly enough both Robertson's fictional ship, the *Titan*, and the *Titanic* met their doom in the month of April. Both vessels also carried too few lifeboats for the number of passengers. In both cases this accounted for the tremendous loss of life which accompanied both disasters.

Many other premonitions of disaster have been reported concerning the *Titanic*. Another writer, W. T. Snead, wrote a short story involving a large ocean liner that also sank in the mid-Atlantic. At the end of the article Snead wrote, "This is exactly what might take place and what will take place, if liners are sent to sea short of boats."

Later when Snead was the editor of a magazine, he wrote another story in which a liner collided with an iceberg. In Snead's story the only surviving passenger was rescued by a White Star liner called the *Majestic*. At that time there was an actual ship called the *Majestic* and the captain was Edward J. Smith. Smith was captain of the *Titanic* when it struck an iceberg in 1912.

While the *Titanic* was being built Snead visited a psychic who told him that travel would be dangerous in the month of April, 1912.

Shortly before the sailing of the *Titanic*

Snead visited another psychic who told him of his dream. In his dream the psychic saw hundreds of people struggling in the water. Snead was one of them.

Despite all of these warnings W. T. Snead sailed on the *Titanic* and died.

There were other predictions, too. On the Isle of Wight, Mr. and Mrs. Marshall and their family were standing on the roof of their home to watch the maiden voyage of the *Titanic*. The Isle of Wight lies off the southern coast of England and Mr. and Mrs. Marshall wished to get a good view of the great White Star liner after it had left the British port of Southampton. The date was April 10, 1912.

For no apparent reason, Mrs. Marshall suddenly began shouting, "That ship is going to sink before it reaches America."

Her husband tried to reassure her that the *Titanic* was unsinkable, but Mrs. Marshall had reached a near hysterical state.

"Don't stand there staring at me!" she shouted. "Do something! I can see hundreds of people struggling in the icy waters! Are you going to let them drown?"

In New York City a woman awoke from a vivid dream. In her dream she could see her mother in a lifeboat tossing helplessly in the sea. The woman dismissed the dream knowing that her mother was in England and could not possibly be at sea.

Unknown to the woman however, her mother

had decided to surprise her daughter and had booked passage on the *Titanic*. At the exact moment that the New York City woman was having her dream, her mother was in the lifeboat from which she was eventually rescued.

Thirty-three-year-old Colen Macdonald was an experienced naval engineer who had logged many miles aboard ship. Macdonald was offered the job as second engineer on the *Titanic*. A strange feeling that the *Titanic* would meet disaster caused Macdonald to refuse the position. The man who took his place was killed in the disaster.

On April 14, 1912, Captain Smith of the *Titanic* received several warnings of icebergs in the North Atlantic. But for Captain Smith and many others, the beginning of the twentieth century marked a period of time in which the advancements in science gave man a feeling of superiority over the forces of nature. Captain Smith had been told that the *Titanic* was unsinkable and like so many others he was convinced that nothing could harm his ship.

At two o'clock on the morning of April 15, 1912, the mighty *Titanic* sank in the North Atlantic and 1,502 people drowned. Most of the disaster victims could have been saved but like the fictional *Titan* no one thought it necessary to have lifeboat space for each passenger.

Could the assassination of President Kennedy and the sinking of the *Titanic* have been prevented? Perhaps they could. In 1966, in London, England, the Central Premonitions Bureau was formed. Its main function was to record premonitions and dreams of impending disasters and to warn those involved. A similar organization called the Central Premonitions Registry was formed several years later in New York City.

But perhaps man would rather not know his future, or at any rate, would disregard warnings and plunge ahead like Captain Smith of the *Titanic*, confident that he is in control of his own destiny.

The Search for Ancient Mysteries

Who built the massive pyramids of Egypt? By what power was early man able to hoist several hundred stone blocks, some of which weighed over 200 tons, more than two miles above sea level, to build the pre-Incan fortress of Sacsahuaman high in the Andes Mountains? Who can explain the Iron Pillar that dates to 5000 B.C. in New Delhi, India, and is made of an alloy that has never rusted. Modern people can not duplicate this alloy.

Did ancient people, with the help of beings from another world, build these and other structures that we have no way of adequately explaining? Did ancient astronauts from some distant planet come to earth many centuries ago and help construct the amazing wonders that still stand today?

The clues are there and are causing scientists to reevaluate some of our theories concerning ancient people. Writers like Erich Von Daniken in his famous book *Chariots of the Gods* have stirred our imaginations. Many of Von Daniken's theories lack factual evidence, but there is no denying that the study of ancient people must be looked at in a totally new light. Let's look at some examples from the ancient world.

Easter Island is a lonely little island 2,350 miles from the coast of Chile in the Atlantic Ocean. The island is a tiny speck, containing only 64 square miles of barren, rocky land. But what mysteries the island holds for the modern world!

Early European explorers at the beginning of the eighteenth century were amazed to see hundreds of enormous stone heads, some standing and some lying on the ground, when they waded ashore. Closer examination revealed that the heads were made of steel-hard volcanic rock. The statues were 33 to 66 feet high with one unfinished statue measuring 164 feet. Many of the statues weighed as much as 50 tons!

The mystery of Easter Island was twofold. First, why were the statues built and secondly, how did early man, possessing only rudimentary tools, manage to haul the rock used to build the statues and then raise them into an upright position?

Erich Von Daniken and others have suggested that the statues were built under the direction of astronauts from another planet, and that the statues are actually memorials to these visitors. Von Daniken points to the fact that there are no trees on Easter Island. This would have made it impossible to move the statues on wooden sleds or rollers. Also the island could not support the thousands of workers necessary for the building of the statues. Crops grow poorly on the island, making the feeding and housing of a large work force impossible.

In addition, the natives living on the island today, although knowing nothing of the construction of the statues, call their island "The Land of the Bird Men." A legend passed down orally from generation to generation tells of flying men who came to Easter Island many centuries ago. This legend is confirmed by sculptures found of flying men with large staring eyes like those on the larger statues.

Many archaeologists, however, believe that the Islanders were Polynesian in origin. Recently deciphered wooden tablets found at the base of the giant statues indicate this. Most likely the island was originally settled in 1300 B.C. by natives from the Society Islands which were then overpopulated.

The stone heads represent ancestors of these early natives. The statues were moved and erected by using cables made of raffia and other vegetable fibers and were hoisted by means of inclined planes made of rocks and sand.

But perhaps the secret of Easter Island will never be known. The giant statues remain, waiting as the legends say, for the return of the ancient astronauts, the Bird Men, who helped build them.

South America and Central America contain many mysteries that modern people cannot explain. The enormous structures built by the Mayan and Aztec cultures of Central America are impressive. Pyramids in Central America indicate possible links between the cultures of Central America and Egypt. But the most impressive wonder of archaeology is found in what is modern Bolivia. It is the ancient city of Tiahuanaco.

Tiahuanaco has been called the oldest city in the world. The city was already a ruin when Spanish explorers conquered the Inca Empire in the fifteenth century.

But despite the fact that the city is in ruins, there is evidence that Tiahuanaco was once one of the greatest cities in the world. It was the center of the vast empire of Peru and probably the source of all the other great civilizations of Central and South America. Parts of buildings still remain, built of Andean granite cut and ground to a smooth finish. The walls were built of blocks so precise that no mortar was needed to join them together. Each block was notched so that it interlocked with the block below and beside it. No one knows how the blocks, some of which weigh 100 tons, could have been lifted and fitted into place.

The most impressive sight in Tiahuanaco today is the famous Gate of the Sun. The Gate of the Sun is actually an archway carved out of one gigantic piece of granite. The name was given to the archway by the Incas in honor of their sun god, but the gate is much older. On the Gate of the Sun are carved many intriguing designs. Row upon row of manlike birds can be seen. A figure wearing an elaborate headdress with several tears coming from its eyes is known as the Weeping God. Why is the god weeping? No one knows. Von Daniken and others have identified other carvings on the Gate of the Sun. Among these are helmeted space travelers and space ships.

The wonder of Tiahuanaco is that it was built in the first place. The city was built at an altitude of over 13,000 feet on the shores of Lake Titicaca. This altitude is above the tree line. Few crops can grow to the height. Why would anyone build a city at such an elevation?

Once again those who believe that ancient astronauts helped construct Tiahuanaco point to the fact that the area would be an ideal landing site for beings from another planet. Its elevation would make it free from germs. The flatness of the area and the still, deep waters of gigantic Lake Titicaca also would make an ideal landing place.

Other scientists believe that at one point Tiahuanaco was much lower in elevation. Somehow, as the Andes Mountains were formed, the entire region was raised by pressure from below. But whatever the answer, Tiahuanaco remains a city of mystery.

West of Tiahuanaco, near the Pacific coastline of Peru, is the ancient city of Nazca. On an elevated platform 1,200 feet high is what some claim to be the remains of an ancient airport. The "airport" can only be appreciated if viewed from the air. At a sufficient height a viewer can see the outlines of a bird, a spider, a fish, a jaguar, and the legendary firebird. The figures are estimated to be about 150 yards long.

More amazing, however, are the series of lines that run in various directions. Some of the lines are parallel while others intersect. The lines could not be roads since they end suddenly and seem to have no logical purpose.

Another possibility is that the lines have astronomical significance. Dr. Paul Kozak of Long Island University made an important discovery in 1941. Sighting along one of the lines on June 22, the day of the winter solstice

In the southern hemisphere, he noticed that the line pointed exactly to the sun as it touched the horizon. Dr. Kozak was standing on a solstice line.

Thus, the lines of Nazca could be a kind of giant astronomical map. But there is no denying that viewed from the air the lines do resemble an airfield. Once again we are baffled by the ingenuity of an ancient people.

Stonehenge, located on the Salisbury Plains in Wilshire, England, is another fascinating study in the continuing mystery of ancient people.

Stonehenge consists of a series of circles made of large blocks of stone. The entire circle which is 100 feet in circumference consists of 30 blocks of gray sandstone each 30 feet long and weighing approximately 28 tons. A continuous circle of smaller blocks was laid on top of them. Inside was a circle of about 60 blue stones. Inside this circle were two other sets of stones. These were in the shape of two horseshoes, one inside the other and opening toward the northeast. Near the inner horseshoe was a flat block of sandstone 16 feet long, which was probably an altar and may have once stood upright.

Early researchers felt that Stonehenge was probably a place of worship. This may have been true at one time. In 1952, underground holes were discovered beneath some of the stones. These holes, which may have been ritual pits, contained charcoal bits. Carbon dating indicated that the charcoal was burned around 1800 B.C.

However, Gerald Hawkins, an American scientist, recently came forth with an interesting theory. Using a computer, Hawkins proved that Stonehenge was actually a sort of prehistoric computer used to predict solar and lunar eclipses. Most scientists who read Hawkins's research agreed with his findings. It had taken a modern computer to discover an ancient computer.

But who built such a computer? Inhabitants of the area were simple people hardly capable of constructing such a sophisticated device.

Stonehenge, like many other mysteries of ancient times, remains unexplained. There are other mysteries. There is in existence a map which is thousands of years old. This map shows the Mediterranean and the Dead Sea region. The map shows the coastlines of North and South America and even Australia. The map even shows the topography of Antarctica which was unknown to us until 1952, when echo sounding devices outlined the surface features. The ancient map is drawn with the areas away from the center becoming more and more distorted. Such a map could only have been drawn from the sky!

There are 250 billion stars in our Milky

Way Galaxy. There are perhaps 100 billion galaxies in the universe. Is it possible, then, that in this vast expanse our Earth is the only planet with intelligent life?

Von Daniken's theories are not so unbelievable. The people of ancient times may have been visited by astronauts from another galaxy with a technology far more advanced than our own. The clues are there. Reports of flying saucers may indicate that the ancient visitors are watching us, waiting once again for the right time and place to return.

The Christmas Miracle

Colonel Julio Ferradas of the Uruguayan Air Force had an uneasy feeling in the pit of his stomach. A twenty-year veteran with over 5,000 miles of flying experience shouldn't have been bothered by the prospects of flying over the Andes Mountains. Yet there was always a certain thrill, an uneasiness, at crossing the huge mountain range, and as Colonel Ferradas watched his co-pilot, Lieutenant Dante Lagurara, direct the American-built Fairchild F-227 toward the foothills of the Andes Mountains, the old feeling of apprehension hit him once again.

There was something that Colonel Ferradas

didn't like about the entire flight. Atmospheric conditions over the Andes had already caused a delay in flight plans. The delay had failed to dim the enthusiasm of his passengers, however. From within the cabin Colonel Ferradas could hear the happy voices of his 48 passengers most of whom were members of the Old Christians rugby team. The Old Christians, along with their supporters, were on their way from Montevideo, Uruguay, to Santiago, Chile. The team would compete against the Chilean National rugby team. The journey duplicated a trip which the team had made in 1971. At that time the Old Christians had won the rugby championship of Uruguay and the trip to Chile had been a complete success. Now, two years later, many of the same group along with several new members hoped to duplicate the success of the previous journey.

Colonel Ferradas, however, seemed unable to share in the merriment from within the cabin of his plane. He knew that weather conditions over the Andes were subject to sudden violent changes. Often, hot currents of air passing over the dry, almost desert-like regions in Argentina would rise to meet the icy winds which blew in from the Pacific. This often caused cyclonic-like winds which could destroy any airplane no matter how skilled the pilot. As Colonel Ferradas watched Lieutenant Lagurara, he knew that his fears should have been groundless. The Fairchild was practically new. In addition it was equipped with the latest in directional epuipment, including an Automatic Direction Finder and other even more sophisticated devices. Finally, his co-pilot Lieutenant Lagurara, though not as experienced as the colonel, was perfectly capable of piloting the Fairchild under most conditions.

Plans for the flight called for the Fairchild to proceed across the Planchon Pass, one of several passes through the Andes. Although passing through the Planchon Pass would take longer, the journey was considered safer than some of the more direct routes.

With all of these safety factors then, Colonel Ferradas should have been able to sit back and enjoy the journey. But as the plane passed the dry, flat region of western Argentina, the massive Andes rose in front of the Fairchild. The sight never failed to thrill Colonel Ferradas and any other pilot who had to cross the second highest mountain range in the world. Soon the flat land gave way to the foothills of the Andes. Then the Fairchild began to climb above an area known as the Cordilla, a region of solid rock without trees or vegetation.

At 13,000 feet the snow line became visible. The Fairchild was now cruising at 18,000 feet toward the Planchon Pass at a speed of 210 knots. A tailwind that often reached 60 knots accompanied the Fairchild.

Below them the two airmen could see that the mountains were now almost completely covered with snow that they knew was sometimes 100 feet deep. Still everything was going routinely and Lieutenant Lagurara radioed Air Traffic Control in Santiago that soon his plane would be over the Planchon Pass.

Then suddenly the trailing winds shifted and in a matter of seconds the plane was heading into a strong head wind. Lieutenant Lagurara slowed the plane down to 180 knots. Then the plane hit a cloud formation causing the craft to shake violently. Lieutenant Lagurara switched on the sign to the passengers within the cabin to fasten their safety belts.

Inside the cabin there was little panic. The high-spirited boys refused to become alarmed. Instead they passed a rugby ball around the cabin and shouted "Ole! Ole!" each time the plane would rise or fall. Suddenly, however, the Fairchild hit an air pocket and plunged several hundred feet. The descent brought the plane out of the cloud formation into the clear blue sky. Lieutenant Lagurara and Colonel Ferradas were shocked to see before them the jagged edge of a mountain no more than ten feet from the wing tip of the plane. Lieutenant Lagurara tried desperately to gain altitude but it was hopeless. Suddenly the right wing hit the side of the mountain with an ear-shattering crash. The wing was torn loose, flying over the fuselage and cutting off the tail of the plane. Out into the air flew three of the boys as well as the plane's steward and the navigator. Then the left wing broke loose. There was nothing now that the horrified officers of the plane could do. The Fairchild was out of control, crashing on its belly down the slope of the snow-covered mountain. Five more boys were sucked out of the back end of the plane into the frigid air.

Finally the Fairchild began to slow down. It stopped and for a moment there was complete silence. From within the cabin of the plane came the moans of the survivors. The crash had caused some of the seats to break loose, crushing the legs of many of the passengers. Many were in worse condition. One passenger had been struck with the plane's propellor. He died within minutes after the crash.

For several moments there was little movement from within the plane. The survivors seemed too stunned, too dazed by the tragedy. The Fairchild had crashed on the side of a mountain at an altitude of 11,500 feet. It was in the Andes close to the borderline between Chile and Argentina. The plane had entered a world of towering mountain peaks and snow-filled valleys. It was a world of bitter cold in which the temperature sometimes plunged to seventy-five degrees below zero. Avalanches could inundate an entire airplane. Very few people had ever set foot in this alien world and for a moment the survivors seemed to be doomed.

But then the strongest instinct of all, the will to survive, overcame the shock of the crash and the hopelessness of the situation. From within the plane the living began to stir. Marcelo Pérez, captain of the rugby team, took it upon himself to begin rescue operations. Roberto Canessa and Gustavo Zerbino, two medical students, volunteered their services. With Pérez they moved among the passengers, trying to free those trapped by the broken seats. The rescue team soon discovered that the survivors were in pitiful condition. Broken bones were common and many of the wounded suffered from internal injuries and severe lacerations. Adding to their miseries were the bitter cold and the fact that most of the survivors were dressed only in summer sport coats.

Slowly, Canessa and Zerbino made their way through the plane. The two medical students were shocked by what they saw. Fernando Parrado's face was covered with blood and bruises and the two thought that he was dead. A young man came up to Zerbino with a severe stomach wound. As calmly as he could, Zerbino tried to reassure the young man. Zerbino found some cologne which he used as a disinfectant and pushed the exposed tissues back into the opening. The young man lived.

For Zerbino and Canessa the demands for aid were far beyond their capabilities. Zerbino had attended only one year of medical school. Canessa was in his second year but had completed only half of the necessary courses. Many of the steps taken by the two young men were makeshift operations performed with inadequate tools or equipment.

As the survivors slowly began to untangle, they saw a sight which made them realize the hopelessness of their situation. Above them they could see Carlos Valeta, one of those who had fallen out of the back of the plane staggering down the mountainside toward them. Valeta seemed dazed and blinded by the snow. Quickly the snow grew deeper around him. Then Valeta disappeared in a valley of snow, never to be seen again.

The crash of the Fairchild had occurred at 3:30 p.m. A light snow was beginning to fall and in a few short hours night would engulf the mountains. Desperately, the survivors, led by team captain Marcelo Pérez, began to make their way toward the cabin of the plane, hoping to make radio contact with the outside. What they saw shocked them. Colonel Ferradas was dead. Lieutenant Lagurara was still alive but in terrible condition. The rescuers tried desperately to get the radio to work but without success. As they turned to leave they found that Lieutenant Lagurara was dead.

The first night in the plane was spent in an atmosphere of panic and hysteria. A large hole in the back of the plane where the tail had been exposed the survivors to the howling wind and bitter cold. This together with the cries and moans of the injured made the night seem like an eternity.

Daylight found the Fairchild half buried in snow in the middle of the Andes. Canessa, Zerbino, and Pérez were now joined by Liliana Methol, who added her abilities. The small group gathered the supplies that were available. They found three bottles of wine, a bottle of whiskey, and other small amounts of alcoholic beverages. The food supply consisted of eight bars of chocolate, some dates and plums, a box of salted crackers, several bottles of jam, and other small amounts of candy and crackers.

Twenty-eight survivors had to share in these meager supplies. For lunch each person was issued a square of chocolate and a deodorant cap filled with wine.

On the second day, the condition and spirit of the survivors began to show a slight improvement. That morning a plane flew over as the survivors shouted and waved their arms. Later that day another plane passed over and seemed to tip its wings as if the pilot had spotted the Fairchild. But the survivors could not have known the hopelessness of being spotted from above. The treacherous mountain peaks made it impossible for any rescue team to fly very low. In addition, the Fairchild appeared as a tiny speck to any rescue plane. This, coupled with the fact that the plane had a white roof, meant that it would have been sheer luck for any rescue plane to spot the survivors in the vast expanse of snow.

By the second day Pérez had organized the survivors into groups. One group consisted of a medical team composed of Canessa, Zerbino, and Liliana Methol. The younger boys formed another group. They were put in charge of keeping the cabin of the plane clean. The third group were the water makers. At first this group made slow progress, attempting to gather the melting snow into bottles. Then Adolfo Strauch discovered that by using aluminum foil from the back of one of the plane's seats as a spout, he could melt the snow much more quickly and put it into bottles.

By the fourth day, the condition of the survivors was considerably improved. Many of the wounds had begun to heal. The most remarkable recovery of all was made by Fernando Parrado. Parrado had been given up for

Then his will to survive overcame h
and he ate.

Later that day, others followed Canessa
lead and before long the supply was exhausted. As the days passed one by one, the
survivors managed to eat the only food that
was available.

As October ended, a certain degree of
order had been established among the survivors. Each person had his assigned job and
the days passed quickly. Only Liliana Methol
still refused to eat. Her condition deteriorated
rapidly.

Then on October 29 disaster struck once
more. Toward the end of the afternoon a biting wind forced everyone inside the hulk of
the Fairchild. Many of the survivors had fallen
desperately to keep warm de-
h forced its way

dead earlier. Now, however, along with his
remarkable recovery he became obsessed
with a desire to escape from the mountain
tomb and spoke of nothing else.

As the days passed the survivors became
divided as to what their future course of
action should be. Some, like Parrado, were
certain that their only hope lay in trying to
get away. Others were positive that help was
on the way and felt it was foolish to risk their
lives on an expedition that could prove dis-
astrous. Others were certain that if they could
just climb to the top of one of the mountains
that surrounded them they would be able to
spot the green fields of Chile in the distance.
Others thought that their hopes rested in
finding the tail of the Fairchild, containing the
batteries which operated the plane's radio. In
addition the tail contained suitcases holding
much needed clothing and perhaps additional
food supplies.

Thus, on October 17, four men led by
Canessa set out on their first rescue mission.
Seats from the plane attached to their feet
served as crude though effective snowshoes.
For a while the expedition went well, but then
as the climbing grew more difficult the four
realized that they had grown too weak to
endure the conditions they faced. As the air
grew thinner they began to flounder in the
deep snow. With night approaching, the men

27

were forced to turn back, arriving at the Fairchild completely exhausted and in a pitiful condition.

An air of despair hung over the survivors. They now sensed that rescue planes could not find them. They also knew that in their present condition they could not live long on the mountainside. Food supplies were now exhausted. The survivors became tired from even the slightest exertion. Then on the ninth day, Susana Parrado, sister of Fernando Parrado, died. Her death caused great sadness among the survivors. They had watched as Fernando had tried desperately to keep her alive. Now her death made everyone realize the total helplessness of their situation.

On the tenth day Roy Harley found a transistor radio which was in working condition. Unable to believe what he heard, Harley learned that rescue operations had been called off. The survivors were on their own.

For several days now the survivors had talked in small groups of a plan for survival that no one was willing to say out loud. Those still alive had eyed the dead bodies that lay all around them. They knew that the bodies buried in the snow were perfectly preserved. They knew also that the dead bodies represented their only hope for survival. In small groups they had discussed the possibility of eating the flesh of their dead comrades. In

this way they could gather strength desperate attempt at escape.

It was a desperate plan conceive perate circumstances. Finally, Robe nessa brought it into the open. argued that the bodies represented fo would keep them alive. Zerbino stresse if he died he would want the others to us body for their survival. Canessa said th was the moral obligation of everyone alive to survive, using whatever means w at their disposal.

Many were shocked at the idea. Lilian Methol, the only woman still alive, argue that she could not eat human flesh no matter how desperate her condition. Others argued with her, stressing the moral implications of the act.

mained calm were able to survive. Others overcome by panic smothered to death or were crushed by the weight of the snow. Before long the body of Marcelo Pérez, the team captain and one of the leaders, was discovered. Liliana Methol was also dead.

When the final count was made the survivors were horrified to find that eight more of their group had died in the avalanche. Only nineteen now survived.

That night was the most miserable that any of the survivors had spent in the Andes. They were cold and wet and outside a blinding blizzard howled. By morning everyone knew that their only chance of survival lay in setting forth on an escape mission out of the Andes. The survivors decided on a desperate scheme. Parrado, Canessa, and Antonio Vizintín set forth on an exploratory mission seeking the best means of escape. The three made rapid progress, as their rugby boots gripped the hard surface of the frozen snow. After several hours of marching, the men were amazed to see in front of them the tail of the Fairchild which had become separated in the crash.

It was a joyous moment for the men. Inside the tail they found suitcases packed with clothing, some rum, several cartons of cigarettes, but more important, they found the batteries which provided power for the Fairchild's radio.

It was with great excitement that the three men returned to the Fairchild, but their joy was short-lived. Lacking the technical knowledge needed, the survivors found it impossible to get the radio working. Once again the men knew that they had wasted valuable time. The trip to the tail had drained the strength of the three. In addition, the precious supply of food was dwindling rapidly.

As the end of November approached, each survivor knew that there was no help coming from anywhere and that no more time could be wasted. They had spent almost two months in indescribable conditions. They had reached the end of their endurance both physically and emotionally. Then Ron Harley became ill and the men knew that he was too weak to last long. The men whom Harley had dug out of the snow when the avalanche had struck knew that without him they wouldn't be alive, and they wanted to repay the debt they owed him.

On the morning of December 12, Parrado, Canessa, and Vizintín arose at 3:30 a.m. They packed food for fifteen days. The other men donated their warmest clothing. Each of the three wore several pairs of trousers, two or three sweaters, a jacket, and the best rugby boots. They wore homemade sunglasses which would be an absolute necessity in cutting down on the glare from the snow.

Each man carried walking sticks made from the plane's aluminum tubing, snowshoes made from seat cushions, and a sleeping bag made from the plastic insulation of the plane. In addition, all three had been given special privileges for the past week. All had been excused from working and they were given extra food rations in order to build up their strength for the ordeal they faced.

The initial objective was to climb the mountain to the east. The men hoped that from this vantage point they would get a view of the green valleys of Chile. For a while the men made good time over the frozen snow, but then the sun came up and the snow became soft. Before long every step was agonizing. As they climbed higher and higher the air became more difficult to breathe. The men in the fuselage below watched as the small rescue team became three tiny specks, making their way up the side of the mountain.

For three days the men climbed. Then Parrado, who had forged ahead of the others, reached the summit. The sight that he saw shocked him. He could see no green valleys. Instead he could see only an endless expanse of mountains, stretching as far as the eye could see.

For a moment complete despair descended on the rescue team. But for Parrado there was no turning back. The three decided that

Vizintín would give Parrado and Canessa his supply of food and return to the plane. Parrado and Canessa hoped that with the additional food supply they would be able to reach civilization. It was a desperate gamble that had to be taken.

The next day Canessa and Parrado continued climbing to a higher peak. Then Canessa, possessed of keen eyesight, made an important discovery. Far in the distance he saw what appeared to be the path of a river winding through the mountains. The men knew that if they could locate the river they could possibly follow it to its source and rescue.

After a day of rest on the mountaintop the men began walking toward the west. Descending the mountains was dangerous as the melting snow had exposed jagged rocks. At one point Parrado who now seemed to possess almost superhuman strength no doubt caused by his fanatical desire to escape, made a toboggan out of his seat cushions. Using the aluminum pole as a break, Parrado began to fly down the side of the mountain. Before long he was crashing headlong at a speed that he later estimated at 60 miles an hour. He went out of control and crashed into a snowbank at the bottom which saved his life.

On the sixth day of their journey the men

came upon a small stream. They drank thirstily from the stream, the first fresh water that they had in over two months. They began to follow the stream and they came upon some moss. Canessa, near the point of exhaustion, crammed the moss into his mouth and ate it. It was the first sign of vegetation that they had seen in 65 days.

Parrado was now in a frenzy to continue but he knew that his friend could not go on. The two slept well that night, knowing that perhaps the next day they might come across signs of life.

The following morning the men continued to follow the tiny stream. By this time Canessa was so completely exhausted that Parrado was forced to help him. The stream soon became larger. Then it was joined by other streams and soon the stream became a sizable river. They had come upon the headwaters of the Azufre River.

There was no stopping now. They came to the end of a long valley and were greeted by a sight which was like paradise to them. In front of them were lush green trees, bushes, grasses, and yellow and purple flowers. For the boys it was a moment of supreme joy and they prayed to God in thanksgiving for delivering them from the frozen Andes.

On the eighth day the men discovered an empty soup can, the first sign of civilization.

Then later Canessa spotted a horseshoe and then he could see cows grazing in the distance.

On the next day, the ninth day since the boys had left the Fairchild, they saw a sight that they had prayed for. On the other side of the river they saw a lone horse and rider. Later that same day they saw three men on horseback. The men waved frantically to the horsemen but all they could hear above the roar of the river were the words "tomorrow." Then the horsemen disappeared.

On the tenth day after leaving the Fairchild, a horseman rode toward Parrado and Canessa on their side of the river. The horseman greeted them with great reluctance and then the boys realized that their condition must have been shocking. But the horseman had in his possession what the boys valued above everything — food. Never had any food tasted so good.

Later the men were taken to a modest workman's hut where they ate four plates of beans each, cooked macaroni with scraps of meat, and large quantities of bread and milk. When they could eat no more, the boys slept. It was midday December 21, seventy days since the Fairchild crashed in the Andes.

The greatest survival story of modern times had ended. Within days the remaining men were rescued by helicopter from the mountains under the direction of Parrado and Canessa. Sixteen young men had survived.

News of the rescue of the sixteen survivors from the Andes was received with tears of joy by the parents of the men who had survived. Mixed in with the happiness was the realization that many would never return from their graves high in the Andes.

But then the news that the men had eaten human flesh reached a disbelieving public. The instant reaction was one of shock.

Debate raged for months, concerning the cannibalism practiced by the survivors. Some argued that the men hadn't really reached the limit of their endurance when such an act would have been justified. Ironically enough it was discovered that a modern resort hotel closed down for the winter was within five miles of the crash sight. If the men had made an exploratory expedition to the east instead of west, they would have discovered the hotel complete with food supplies and provisions.

But the majority of the public sympathized with the actions of the survivors. Most church authorities stated that the men had not committed a wrong. They reasoned that under the unique circumstances, a person is obligated to survive using any methods available.

Antonio Vizintín, one of the sixteen survivors, expressed the feeling that many of the men could not put into words. "I don't think I have anything to regret and I don't think it was evil. I think we used something without movement, without life, something completely material, with which sixteen human beings could continue to live."

On Christmas Day, 1973, the survivors and their families attended a special mass of thanksgiving in the chapel of Catholic University in Santiago, Chile.

No one knows the private thoughts of the young men gathered together in prayer. No doubt each prayed for the strength to face a questioning world, not all of whom would be kind. But at that moment the thoughts of the men undoubtedly turned to the frozen Andes where so many had died and sixteen had lived.

The Unbelievable Case of Patience Worth

Anyone who investigates unusual phenomena will agree that few stories can match the strange case of Patience Worth. The events that Mrs. John Curran experienced in 1913 have never been fully explained and to this day they remain as mysterious as they did over 50 years ago. Patience Worth was a "spirit" who lived in the time of the Pilgrims, who presumably managed to communicate poems and even entire books to Mrs. John Curran, an ordinary St. Louis housewife. Today these poems and books can still be found on library shelves and bookstores. The story of Patience Worth is far stranger than any fiction ever written.

The story begins on a warm night in 1913.

Mr. and Mrs. John Curran of St. Louis were entertaining friends in their home. They were having fun with a Ouija board which was a popular parlor game at that time. One of the group would ask a question and another person would then hold his hand on the planchette which is a smaller board that sits on top of the Ouija board. The planchette would move about the board and spell out the answer to the question. For most the Ouija board is a harmless game, but there are those who believe that the Ouija board or psychograph can be used for supernatural purposes.

Mrs. Curran was reluctant to experiment with the Ouija board. She didn't care for spiritualism in any form. Her uncle was a Spiritualist and Mrs. Curran disliked the crowd that would gather in his church. But on the night of July 8, 1913, when Mrs. Curran placed her fingers on the planchette, her hand moved effortlessly over the alphabet on the Ouija board and spelled out some words. Mrs. Curran decided to go along with the game in order to keep her friends happy.

But suddenly Mrs. Curran's hand moved quickly over the board and spelled out the words that were to change the course of her entire life. "Many moons ago I lived. Again I come — Patience Worth my name."

The words were strange and those gathered around the Ouija board thought for a moment that Mrs. Curran was playing a trick on them.

Mrs. Curran sat stunned for several minutes. She refused to believe what was happening but she knew that someone was trying to contact her through the medium of the Ouija board.

Several more minutes passed. Then Mrs. Curran placed her fingers on the planchette. Once again Mrs. Curran's hand began moving swiftly over the board and spelled out another message. "Wait, I would speak with thee. If thou shalt live, then so shall I. I make my bread at thy hearth. Good friends, let us be merrie. The time for work is past. Let the tabby drowse and blink her wisdom to the firelog."

They were strange words from another time and place. Mrs. Curran and her friends didn't know what to think of the messages.

The small group tired to find out who Patience Worth was, but she was reluctant to talk about her past.

Slowly, in subsequent sessions, some of the pieces began to fall into place. Mrs. Curran learned that Patience was born in England. About the year she was uncertain. Once the planchette spelled out the year 1649 and then later spelled out 1694. She had worked in the fields and in the house until she was a young woman. Then she immigrated to America where she had been killed by Indians.

This was all that Mrs. Curran could learn

about Patience Worth's past but in other ways Patience was eager to communicate.

As the months passed the Ouija board gave way to what is known as "automatic writing." In automatic writing Mrs. Curran would completely relax both mentally and physically, with pencil in hand. The pencil would then begin writing the words of Patience Worth communicated directly through her medium, Mrs. Curran.

Later Mrs. Curran did not even use pencil and paper. Instead she would sit completely relaxed in a chair. Then she would feel a slight pressure on the top of her head and the words of Patience Worth would pour forth to be recorded by the people waiting to write down the messages.

It soon became apparent to all that Patience had a keen wit and her communications with Mrs. Curran and others were very humorous. Once a professor trying to learn more of Patience's past life asked her if she had been killed in King Phillip's War and if she knew the name of the Indian who killed her. Patience, refusing to be trapped, answered quickly, "If someone had a sword at thy throat wouldst thee stop to inquire his name?"

In the beginning Patience dictated poems and sayings but as the years passed her dictations became longer and longer. Eventually it wasn't unusual for her to dictate 3,000 words in an hour and a half. At one sitting close to six thousand words were dictated and before long skilled stenographers were hired to record the communications in shorthand. In all, over two million words were transcribed from Patience Worth's first communication and the death of Mrs. Curran twenty-five years later.

Patience Worth's longest work was a complete novel entitled *The Sorry Tale* which was published in 1918 by Henry Holt and Company. The novel was a brilliant work which Patience considered her masterpiece. The book was 640 pages long and was set in Palestine at the time of Christ.

Another of her books, *Hope Trueblood*, told the story of English peasant life in the eighteenth century. Many in her audience were not satisfied with the ending of *Hope Trueblood* so Patience simply changed the final two pages. This book was published in 1918.

In all of her works Patience Worth wrote in the language of the seventeenth century. An American philologist did a word-by-word analysis of "Telka," Patience's greatest poem and discovered that the poem did not contain a single word that entered the language after the time period when Patience lived on Earth.

No adequate explanation of the Patience Worth phenomenon has ever been given.

Some have suggested that Patience Worth was a subconscious personality of Mrs. Curran. But it was also noted that Mrs. Curran was a poor student and dropped out of high school after completing her freshman year. She read very little as a child and had very little interest in history. Concerning her writing ability Mrs. Curran once remarked, "I remember only two attempts, except for some Valentine single verses, to write poetry, and these were when I was about fifteen. They were very poor stuff, and my father was amused, though kind. I never wrote anything in prose but little school compositions."

Mrs. Curran had some musical talent. She played the piano and sang in the church choir. But she was not interested in religion and rarely listened to the sermons.

Others have suggested that Mrs. Curran was very neurotic. But none of her past life gave an indication of any neurotic behavior.

For a period of about fifteen years, Mrs. Curran was visited continually by newspaper and magazine writers. No fewer than 35 scientists visited Mrs. Curran during this period. All of them were convinced that Mrs. Curran was not a fraud, but none of them was ready to admit that Patience Worth was a personality who had lived two centuries ago in England and New England.

Others saw in Patience Worth proof of

the existence of life after death, although Patience would never give any indication of her present state of existence.

Several years before her death Mrs. Curran moved from St. Louis to Santa Monica, California, where she married a retired physician. A few days before the wedding Mrs. Curran received a poem from Patience Worth which was set to music and was sung at the wedding — a gift of love from one old friend to another.

Since the death of Mrs. Curran, occasional magazine articles have alluded to the existence of Patience Worth. Succeeding generations have found it difficult to believe that a spirit could "write" poems and books that were sold in bookstores throughout the world. But mostly Patience Worth has been forgotten.

Perhaps someday, somehow, Patience Worth will return. Someone will hear the words, "Many moons ago I lived. Again I come — Patience Worth my name."

The Killer Bees Are Coming

Is the United States about to be invaded by vicious killer bees that attack animals and people, causing instant death? Should the United States be preparing for an invasion more deadly than any one a foreign country could launch?

In his novel, *Swarm*, author Arthur Herzog tells of a family in upper New York State that was attacked by killer bees. The novel goes on to tell of mass attacks by killer bees all over the country. Soon the killer bees multiply, crippling industry and driving people indoors. The novel culminates in a final attack on New York City by billions of killer bees. It is a gripping story in the best traditions of science fiction.

"But it is only science fiction," is the way most people regard *Swarm* and other books that deal with nature on the rampage. Yet recently the true stories coming from Brazil and other parts of South America give every indication that the events in *Swarm* are not as bizarre as they might seem.

Recently Joaquim de Silva, a seventy-four year old Brazilian farmer, was riding his horse along a highway. Suddenly his horse encountered a swarm of killer bees. The insects immediately attacked the horse. The horse went into a fit of panic throwing de Silva to the ground. While de Silva watched in horror, unable to move because of a broken leg, the insects pursued his horse down the road leaving de Silva. Three days later the horse died from thousands of bee stings.

In another instance, a Brazilian school teacher slapped and killed a killer bee as she was arriving at school one morning. Within minutes thousands of killer bees attacked the teacher while her students watched in horror. Police and neighbors arrived but were driven back by the ferocity of the bees. A force of firemen arrived but their hoses were no match for the bees. Finally the firemen lighted torches and managed to drive away the bees, but by the time they reached the teacher she was dead.

Reports such as these have been coming in

from Brazil for several years now. In one area eighteen persons were killed by killer bee attacks in a two-month period. Bees have killed chickens, dogs, and cows, and will attack virtually anything that moves when the insects are angered sufficiently.

One Brazilian farmer can attest to the fact that the killer bees will attack almost anything. One day while plowing his field on his tractor, he disturbed a nest of bees on the ground. The bees swarmed, forming a huge black cloud in the sky above the farmer. In a state of panic the farmer ran for his life, forgetting that he had his tractor in gear. After running for a good distance, the farmer glanced over his shoulder to see the swarm attacking his tractor which was still rolling along.

The killer bees are actually African bees that were brought into South America in 1956. Brazilian entomologist, Warwick Kerr, had long been aware of the African bees' superior energy and amazing breeding ability. Kerr felt that if he could cross the aggressive African bee with the gentler Italian and German bees, commonly called European bees, he could create a super-bee capable of producing honey in large quantities.

In 1956, Kerr imported forty-eight African queen bees to Brazil. Of the forty-eight, twenty-six survived the trip. Kerr and the other Brazilian scientists were well aware of the bees' ferocity and kept them in their hives by means of queen excluder-barriers with holes big enough to admit worker bees but too small for the queens to get through.

Experiments were progressing well for Kerr and the other Brazilian scientists. But the following year a visiting beekeeper mistakenly removed the queen excluders and all twenty-six of the African queens escaped into the forest.

The African bees multiplied rapidly. Soon they emerged from the forest into the farming country and then invaded smaller villages and towns.

The reputation of the African bees, now called killer bees, quickly spread. Brazilians tried desperately to control the migrating bees. Whenever a hive was found, farmers would burn the hive. Poisons of various types were found which unfortunately killed other living creatures as well as the killer bees.

Brazilian scientists began to learn more about the bees as time went on. They learned that the sting of a single bee was no more lethal than the sting of a European bee. Actually the two bees are very similar in appearance. It is the swarming power of the African bees that makes them so dangerous. Since an ordinary person cannot survive more than 200 bee stings, an attack by several thousands is almost always fatal.

Why the African bees attack in such great

numbers is not entirely clear. Some scientists feel that the African bee is more sensitive to disturbances than the European bee. As a result, when the African bee is disturbed, it may emit an odor signal that calls other bees to the attack. Soon the victim is overwhelmed by enraged bees.

Already the killer bees have conquered and now occupy a territory in South America as large as the United States. The killer bees are moving at a rate of 200 miles a year and at their present rate should enter Central America in about five years.

It is in Central America that scientists hope to stop the killer bees. Parts of Central America such as the Isthmus of Panama are only 28 miles wide. Perhaps here the killer bees could be stopped by pesticides or some other method.

Most scientists feel that the bees can be stopped. They point to other methods that have worked. Efforts to control the African bees in southern Brazil were fairly successful. After their escape in 1957, the bees which spread to the north encountered little opposition. These were the bees which killed animals as well as humans. But in southern Brazil the Africans encountered well-established populations of European bees. Through extensive mixing with the European bees and through the efforts of Brazilian scientists in removing the African queens, the African bees in southern Brazil seem to have lost a great deal of their aggressiveness. The resultant hybrid bee has been what Kerr hoped for when he first imported the African bee — a bee that is harder working, produces more honey, and can pollinate more crops than the European bee.

Scientists have also noted that the African bee thrives best in tropical areas. As a result the killer bees may go no further than the southern part of the United States. In addition there are large colonies of European bees in Costa Rica and Mexico which could diminish the aggressiveness of the African bees. Such a bee could actually be a blessing to American farmers rather than a curse.

But like a mutant in a science-fiction movie, the killer bees move forward and the United States is preparing for their coming. Already bills have been passed in Congress forbidding the importation of African bees with stiff fines and imprisonment attached.

At the present rate of progression the killer bees will not reach the United States for 20 years. But like the sudden bee attack in the book *Swarm*, the bees could arrive any day aboard a ship or plane or even attached to the luggage of an unsuspecting carrier. Some have no doubt that the killer bees are coming. Maybe they are already here.

The Curse of the Pharaohs

On December 19, 1966, in Cairo, Egypt, the Egyptian government's Director of Antiquities, Mohammed Ibrahim, was struck by a car and killed.

Ibrahim had just emerged from a conference with French diplomats at the Ministry of Culture. Ibrahim had fought in vain to halt the decision of the Egyptian government to send relics from the "cursed tomb" of King Tutankhamen to Paris for an exhibition. Earlier Ibrahim had agreed to the decision. But as soon as he had, his daughter was seriously injured in an automobile accident. Shortly afterward Ibrahim began to have dreams that he would die.

At the meeting, Ibrahim was told that his

daughter's accident was merely a coincidence. His dreams were a reaction to the accident. Government officials officially pronounced "The Curse of the Pharaohs" to be only a superstition.

Ibrahim left the meeting convinced that the government officials were right. He gave his permission for the shipment of the relics, and within minutes after leaving the conference Ibrahim was dead.

Was this another in an incredible series of deaths that have occurred since the discovery of King Tutankhamen's Tomb in 1917? Archaeological history was made in 1917 when Howard Carter discovered the unopened tomb of the youthful Egyptian Pharaoh. The discovery of the tomb is a fascinating story in itself. The subsequent story of the curse that accompanied the disturbance of the resting place of King Tutankhamen is an eerie account that had its roots in ancient Egypt over 3,000 years ago.

The story begins in the early part of this century. For years archaeologists had searched the Valley of the Kings, the ancient burial places of the Egyptian Pharaohs. Grave robbers had forced the ancient Pharaoh to abandon the traditional pyramids. Instead, in a large valley on the west bank of the Nile near the city of Thebes, tombs were cut into the rocky face of the cliffs which enclosed the valley. In these tombs were placed the mummies of the Pharaohs and other important personages together with riches beyond belief. The entrance was then sealed in the hope that the graves would be safe from grave robbers for eternity.

An understanding of the process of mummification, the building of the pyramids, and the elaborate cliff tombs in the Valley of the Kings can be grasped only in terms of Egyptian religious beliefs. The urge to build pyramids was rooted in the Egyptian belief that after physical death the soul would continue to exist through eternity. The Egyptians believed in a hereafter which was somewhere beyond earth and sky. In this region lived the dead. Egyptian religious beliefs insisted that in the hereafter the soul would someday be reunited with the body, a body that had to be perfectly preserved to enable the wandering soul to find its way back to its rightful place. This belief led to the practice of mummification as well as the construction of the immense pyramids and cliff dwellings all designed for the preservation of the body.

That the Egyptians went to great lengths to safeguard the bodies of the deceased can be seen today in the presence of the pyramids, eight of which still stand. The Great Pyramid alone is one of the great constructions of all time. For twenty years, 100,000 slave laborers hauled 2,300,000 blocks of stone each weighing 2½ tons as the Great Pyramid rose tier by tier, until it reached a height of 481 feet. All of this effort was expended so that someday the soul of the Pharaoh Cheops could be reunited with his body.

Despite the massive bulk of the pyramids and the intricate passageways that were constructed in order to confuse intruders, grave robbers still managed to gain entry. Over the course of centuries all of the pyramids were pillaged and many of the riches from within were carried off or sold.

Eventually the Pharaohs abandoned the pyramids and had their burial chambers moved to the Valley of the Kings. Here the Pharaohs hoped to remain safe from grave robbers. Into the sides of the cliffs they built elaborate apartment-like dwellings. Each room was filled with riches, all of which would be used in the next life. In one of the rooms would be placed the mummified body of the Pharaoh surrounded by his most precious possessions.

Mummification was also used to preserve the body for use in later life. It was an involved process in which the internal organs of the deceased were removed and replaced by sawdust or a similar material. The body was then chemically dried out and finally wrapped tightly in linen cloth. This process together with the dry Egyptian climate usually preserved the bodies for thousands of years.

The final step was the placing of a curse on the tomb of the deceased Pharaoh. The curse, like the other measures, was designed to frighten away would-be intruders, thus preserving the remains for use in the after life.

It was generally believed that the Valley of the Kings had been thoroughly searched and that no more tombs could possibly be found. But in 1902 American archaeologist Theodore Davis received permission from Egyptian authorities to excavate in the Valley of the Kings. Davis managed to unearth several important discoveries, including the tombs of several prominent Pharaohs. Unfortunately, in every case ancient grave robbers had taken most of the treasures from the sites.

One of Davis' assistants was a young British archaeologist named Howard Carter. Despite evidence to the contrary, Carter believed that there were still important discoveries to be made in the Valley of the Kings. He knew that the tomb of the boy Pharaoh, Tutankhamen, had never been discovered and he felt certain that somewhere in the Valley of the Kings his tomb would be found.

In 1914, Howard Carter began excavations for the tomb of Tutankhamen. Earlier, Carter had met George Herbert, fifth Earl of Carnarvon, who agreed to finance Carter's work.

The union of Carter and Lord Carnarvon was a fortunate one. Carter was a painstaking archaeologist possessed of infinite patience. Each digging, each clue, was inspected to the most minute detail by Carter. He was a professional in every sense of the word.

Lord Carnarvon, on the other hand, was a wealthy playboy interested in horses and fast cars. Several years before meeting Carter, Carnarvon had been seriously injured in an automobile accident in Germany. The accident had left Lord Carnarvon in poor health. The damp English weather bothered Carnarvon, and he hoped that the dry Egyptian climate would be beneficial to his health.

Although Carnarvon could be termed a playboy, he had also been educated in British universities and was interested in the arts. He turned naturally toward archaeology. His early attempts met with little success, however.

Early attempts of the Carter-Carnarvon team also met with little success. However, Carter was confident that the tomb of Tutankhamen was somewhere in the Valley. Periodically small objects such as cups and pottery had been found bearing the name of Tutankhamen, indicating to Carter that the major tomb was still to be found.

Carter centered his search on the floor of the Valley of the Kings. Centuries of excavating had left the floor piled with mounds of debris from previous diggings. Carter's approach was a different one. He felt that the tomb must be under one of the piles. He believed that the steps leading downward would reveal the entrance to the tomb.

On November 4, 1922, with Lord Carnarvon back in England, Carter uncovered a stone step beneath an old workmen's hut. By the afternoon of November 5th, enough rubble had been uncovered to reveal a flight of stairs leading downward. Undoubtedly Carter was onto something big.

The workmen pressed on feverishly with the excitement mounting as the digging progressed. After 12 steps Carter discovered the doorway which was sealed against intruders. On the doorway Carter was overjoyed to find the royal seal of Tutankhamen.

Carter's excitement knew no bounds. He was on the verge of one of the greatest discoveries in archaeological history, but he knew that without Lord Carnarvon present his triumph would not be complete. Quickly he rushed a telegram to Carnarvon that read, "At last have made wonderful discovery in valley — a magnificent tomb with seals intact; re-covered same for your arrival; congratulations."

On November 23, Lord Carnarvon arrived, accompanied by his daughter. On November 24, Carter discovered that the seal had actually been broken once and then resealed again. Possibly grave robbers had actually entered the tomb at one time.

Finally the door was opened revealing a passageway littered with fallen rocks. After several days the workmen managed to clear the thirty-two foot long passageway. At the end was another door bearing the seal of Tutankhamen.

"The decisive moment had arrived," Carter wrote later. "With trembling hands I made a tiny breach in the upper-left-hand corner."

Taking an iron testing rod, Carter poked it through the door and found emptiness on the other side. He lit several candles to insure against poisonous gases. Then the hole was enlarged.

Everyone gathered around as Carter peered into the hole. At first he could see little. Then his eyes became accustomed to the darkness. The others waited breathlessly for what seemed to be an eternity. Finally Carnarvon asked impatiently, "Can you see anything?"

"Yes, wonderful things," replied Carter excitedly.

Opening the door, the group found a room filled with beautiful objects. "Surely never before in the history of excavation had such an amazing sight been seen as the light of our torch revealed to us," wrote Carter. Carter had discovered the antichamber of the royal tomb. In the room were golden couches, beautiful shrines, four chariots covered with gold, vases of alabaster, and countless objects made of solid gold. The light from Carter's electric lamp also revealed a golden snake and two royal statues facing each other with protective sacred cobras on their heads.

It was soon obvious to Carter and Carnarvon that the tomb of Tutankhamen was not to be found in the antichamber. Between the two statues they could see another sealed door leading undoubtedly to another chamber. This had to contain the coffin of Tutankhamen, they reasoned.

For Howard Carter and Lord Carnarvon the urge to continue must have been tremendous, but then Carter did something that only a trained archaeologist could understand. He ordered the objects from the antichamber and another smaller side chamber that they had found to be carefully removed. Carter realized that the priceless objects now exposed to the air were in danger of decomposition and as a skilled scientist he wished to take every precaution to insure that the objects were handled with care. He then ordered the door to the tomb sealed again and a twenty-four hour guard was placed in the entranceway.

One of the objects removed from the antichamber was a clay tablet. Inscribed on the tablet was the message, "Death will slay on his wings whoever disturbs the peace of the Pharaohs." Mysteriously the tablet disappeared shortly afterward, never to be found again. In the back of a statue at the far end of the antichamber another inscription was found. It read: "It is I who drive back the robbers of the tomb with the flames of the desert. I am the protector of Tutankhamen's grave." Many references to these inscriptions were to be made in the years to come.

Finally on February 17, 1923, Carter and twenty followers entered the burial chamber. The wonders of the antichamber paled by comparison to what the men found within. There in the midst of a group of gold plated shrines rested the coffin of Tutankhamen.

The youthful Pharaoh, only eighteen at the time of his death, was enclosed in three coffins each inside the other. The first two were made of wood carved with beautifully decorated gold leaf. The third was made of solid gold so heavy that it took four men to raise the lid. Inside rested the mummy of the young king, his head covered with a portrait mask of pure gold. His fingers and toes were also covered with gold.

But then Carter saw something that touched him deeply. On the forehead of the young Pharaoh was a wreath of flowers undoubtedly placed their by his equally youthful queen. Somehow the flowers still retained a touch of their color. This simple touch made the passing of 3,000 years seem like a very short period of time for Howard Carter, and he began to realize that amid the splendor and gold of ancient Egypt there also existed the love of one human being for another.

News of the discovery of the tomb of King Tutankhamen, or King Tut as he was popularly called, spread throughout the world. Soon the sight was visited by thousands of tourists. Some were critical of Carter for having disturbed the resting place of the dead. Others talked of the tablet bearing the inscription, "Death will slay on his wings whoever disturbs the peace of the Pharaohs."

Then suddenly, only six months after the opening of the tomb, Lord Carnarvon died. Lord Carnarvon had cut himself shaving and was bitten by a mosquito. He contracted a high fever from which he never recovered. Shortly after the death of Lord Carnarvon, all of the lights in Cairo suddenly went out. The electric company had no explanation for the occurrence. Back in London, Lord Carnarvon's fox terrier suddenly began to howl, sat up on his hind legs, and fell over dead.

Shortly after, Arthur Mace, an American archaeologist, fell into a coma and died in the same hotel as Lord Carnarvon. Mace had been present at the opening of the tomb. Doctors had no explanation for Arthur Mace's death.

Lord Carnarvon's death brought an old American friend, George Jay Gould, son of the famous American financier, to Cairo. Gould visited the tomb and the next morning contracted a high fever from which he eventually died.

Another friend of Lord Carnarvon, British industrialist Joel Wool, also visited the tomb. On the ship returning to England he also was stricken with a high fever and later died in England.

Soon after, Archibald Reed, a radiologist who participated in the X-raying of King Tutankhamen, suffered a strange attack of feebleness and in 1924 died upon returning to England.

By 1929 twenty-two people who had been directly or indirectly involved with the tomb had died. Thirteen of the twenty persons who had entered the tomb when it was first opened had died. Among these were Professors Winlock and Foucrat, archaeologists Garry Davies, Harkness, and Douglas Derry, and assistant archaeologists, Astor and Callender.

Lord Carnarvon's wife, Lady Almina, died in 1929 of an insect bite.

The death of Carter's secretary, Richard Bethell, in 1929 set off a series of events that was the strangest of all. Bethell was found in bed, dead of circulation collapse. When his eighty-seven-year-old father, Lord Westbury, heard the news he plunged from the seventh floor of his London home. Then on the way to the cemetery his hearse ran over and killed a little boy.

Finally in 1966, Mohammed Ibrahim died trying to prevent another disturbance of the remains of King Tutankhamen.

What are some reasons for the uncanny string of deaths following the excavation of the tomb of King Tutankhamen? Is there really a curse?

Pure coincidence would account for many of the deaths. Those who point to this simple explanation also point to the fact that Howard Carter lived to the age of sixty-seven. If there was a curse, certainly Carter should have been the number one victim.

Sir Wallace Budge, a world famous archaeologist who dug up the mummies of several pharaohs, died at the age of seventy-seven. Another archaeologist, Sir Flanders Petrie, died at the age of eighty-nine and Professor Percy Newbery who entered the tomb lived until 1949 when he died at the age of eighty. Then what also of the grave robbers who consistently managed to defy the curse?

Recently, several scientists have advanced the theory that the deaths could be blamed on a fungus or microbe capable of surviving for thousands of years inside the tomb. Since many of the victims died of high fevers contracted from a mysterious source, this theory bears watching. Others, however, point out that the tombs are too dry to sustain life in any form.

The final chapter of the story of King Tutankhamen, more mysterious than anything that has happened in this century, is still to be written. Tutankhamen's mummy had been X-rayed shortly after his discovery. But in 1963, Dr. Ronald Harrison of Liverpool, England, using more advanced techniques, examined the body again. Harrison found that beyond doubt the young Pharaoh had been killed by a violent blow to the head. Dr. Harrison had uncovered a murder mystery 3,000 years old.

The Human Fly

No one who has ever stood at the top of a tall building such as the Sears Building in Chicago or the Empire State Building or one of the twin towers of the World Trade Center in New York will ever forget the feeling. Far below, the viewer can barely see automobiles and buses crawling like tiny ants. Even smaller are people, almost microscopic in size. The view inspires a vague feeling of fear. Although safe from falling, the viewer knows that he is separated from death only by a short wall or a wire enclosure.

For anyone who has ever had that feeling, the sight of twenty-seven-year-old George Willig scaling the 1,350 foot tall World Trade Center in New York City on May 26, 1977, was an awe inspiring sight.

Early morning viewers were amazed to see the figure of a slightly built, bearded climber slowly making his way up the side of the South Tower of the World Trade Center. Before long thousands had gathered in the streets below straining their necks as the figure of George Willig grew smaller and smaller.

Few had been awake at 6:30 a.m. when Willig began his climb. Willig arrived in a van with his twenty-two-year-old brother, Stephen, with whom he had begun rock climbing four years earlier. Also accompanying Willig were his friend and rock climbing partner, Jerry Hewitt, and Randy Zeidberg, George's girlfriend, also an accomplished mountain climber.

Willig began working rapidly, hoping to get underway before Port Authority police interrupted his climb. Quickly Willig unpacked the climbing equipment that he had designed and built himself. He was employed as a toy designer by the Ideal Toy Company and had worked on the equipment after working hours. Willig's plan was to use the aluminum channel designed as a guide for window washing scaffolds that ran the entire length of the building. Into this channel Willig would insert a device which was actually a variation of a standard climbing device called an ascendeur. The ascendeurs served as moveable pulleys. Attached to the ascendeurs and to Willig's feet, wrist, and the climber's harness that he wore was a royal-blue nylon rope. The rope went from the ascendeurs through the shoulder and seat harness and acted in the same way as stirrups around the feet. As Willig put his weight on one foot, the ascendeurs, because of the downward weight of Willig's body, would expand and grip firmly into the aluminum channel. At this point the weight could be removed from the other ascendeur, allowing Willig the opportunity to slide it to the next slot in the channel. In this way Willig began "walking" up the side of the 110-story building.

Almost twenty feet after Willig began climbing, Port Authority police learned of his attempt. Willig ignored several officers' orders to come down.

By 7:00 a.m. Willig had reached the twenty-eighth floor and a huge crowd had begun to form at the foot of the World Trade Center to watch. By this time an emergency squad had been dispatched to the scene by the New York City Police Department.

If rescuers had known the preparations that went into George Willig's climb, they would have known that he needed no help. But authorities had become wary of stunts involving the World Trade Center. In August of 1974 Phillipe Petit, a French high wire artist, spent forty-five minutes doing tricks on a tight rope strung between the two buildings. Then in July of 1975, Owen Quinn, a parachutist, jumped from the North Tower, landing unhurt.

Perhaps there is something about the twin towers rising majestically on Manhattan's southern tip that inspires attempts to conquer the sheer height of the two buildings. Only the Sears Building in Chicago is taller. The World Trade Center even seems to have eclipsed the grandeur of the world famous Empire State Building which now ranks in third place among the tallest buildings in the world.

For George Willig the World Trade Center represented a challenge for which he had been preparing for over a year. Five times late at night Willig had tested his equipment. Once he had been caught in the act by a security guard. Willig quickly talked his way out of the situation, telling the guard that he was an architectural engineering student testing a new safety device for window washers.

Often George Willig had walked to the World Trade Center during the year preceding his climb. He would stare up at the building trying to visualize himself actually in the act of climbing. Willig had been climbing mountains for many years. He had scaled peaks in upper New York State and New

Hampshire. Willig had even conquered El Capitan, the sheer rock face in Yosemite Valley in California, one of the most difficult climbing challenges in the world.

George Willig was ready then for the climb which had become a personal challenge to him. By the twenty-fifth floor he knew that he was free of the cherry pickers used by the fire department to rescue people from burning buildings. This had been his main fear, that he would be stopped and forced to earth in this manner before he had really gotten very high.

In the meantime, police had arrested his friends who were shouting encouragement to Willig. They were taken to the Port Authority Police Station in the basement of the building where they were arrested and fingerprinted. Police charged them with being accomplices and questioned them concerning George's sanity.

A police helicopter as well as other helicopters carrying newsmen and photographers were swarming around the building. Network television had been alerted and a breathless early morning audience watched as George Willig inched his way past the fortieth floor, then the fiftieth.

Meanwhile police had made their way to the top of the building. Two officers were then lowered by a motorized scaffold toward

Willig in a rescue mission. It was at this point that Willig gave the crowd a thrill that they would never forget. Seeing the scaffolding equipment approach, Willig uncoiled a 120-foot nylon climbing rope that he carried over his shoulder for exactly such an emergency. Willig then performed a movement known in mountain climbing as a pendulum. Tying the rope to an ascendeur, Willig swung out and away from the building to another aluminum runner where he planned to continue his climb safe from the police. As he swung away from the building, however, his shadow suddenly dropped down the side of the building. The crowd gasped thinking that the shadow was Willig's falling body.

Willig and the two policemen talked for a while from his new position. The policemen were Glen Kildare, a Port Authority policeman, and Dewitt Allen, a New York City policeman, skilled at suicide rescue operations. The policemen became convinced quickly that Willig wasn't crazy. Later Allen recalled the meeting. "I knew right away he wasn't some nut. I asked him if he wanted to come aboard, and then he said no, he was safer where he was. After we assured him that we weren't going to force him off, we got along fine."

As Willig approached the top of the building, the huge crowd began to cheer his every move. Newsmen by the hundreds had gathered on the roof and watched breathlessly as Willig worked his way higher and higher.

Finally at 10:05 a.m., three and a half hours after beginning his climb, George Willig reached the top of the building. Below the crowd and the millions more watching on television cheered and breathed a collective sigh of relief.

At the top, Willig was welcomed by police and newsmen. The police first asked him for his autograph then slapped handcuffs on him and took him to the basement where his friends were being held.

Officers typed up charges of criminal trespassing, disorderly conduct, and reckless endangerment. A representative of the New York City Corporation Counsel arrived to present Willig with a court summons and a claim for $250,000 expenses incurred by the city.

According to Police Commissioner Michael Codd, the department was forced to send eighty men and many pieces of special equipment including a helicopter to the scene.

The next day, however, New York City Mayor Abraham Beame, at a mobbed news conference at City Hall, announced that the city of New York had no desire to prosecute Willig. Instead Mayor Beame announced that Willig would be fined a penny for each floor for a total of one dollar and ten cents. It was the Mayor's way of saluting the young man who had given New York City a thrill it wouldn't soon forget.

Then the inevitable questions began to pour in. "Why did you do it?" was the one asked most often.

"It was a personal challenge," replied Willig. "I just wanted to get to the top."

George Willig seemed amazed by the reaction to his climb. At the news conference he stated, "I'm still amazed at all this hullaballo."

It was obvious that George Willig was a young man interested only in the climb for an inner satisfaction all his own. Some newsmen suggested, however, that Willig may have climbed the building for money or fame.

"I just wanted the prize of climbing it," insisted Willig. "The biggest challenge came from designing the ascendeurs," he said. "Rock climbing is a lot more scary because it's so problematical and precarious. I had solid footing all the way up the building, and my route was predetermined, so I had no decisions to make. That's what's so difficult about rock climbing."

Willig didn't think that the climb was that difficult. But few in the crowd watching him climb the World Trade Center would agree there was *anything* easy about the climb.

Onado's Private War

Lieutenant Hiroo Onado of the Japanese Imperial Army stared through his binoculars, unable to believe the sight before him. From his mountain hideout on the island of Lubang in the Philippine Islands, Onado watched a sight that he would never forget. In front of him an armada of American ships stretched as far as he could see. The date was January 3, 1945. Lieutenant Onado knew that the moment that he had been dreading was at hand. The American invasion of the Philippine Islands had begun.

Despite his apprehension, Lieutenant Onado couldn't help but admire the invasion fleet. Quickly he counted two battleships, four aircraft carriers, four cruisers, and thirty-eight light cruisers and destroyers. Behind these stretched an unending sea of troop transports. A quick count revealed 150 of these. Behind the troop transports innumerable landing craft and subchasers followed, too large in numbers for Onado to even make an estimate. The fleet was headed toward the island of Luzon.

Four years earlier at the beginning of World War II, American forces had been driven from the Philippines when Japanese forces overran the islands of the Pacific. But now the tide had turned, and Lieutenant Onado knew instinctively that the beginning of the end had arrived for the Japanese army in the Philippines.

Onado knew that he still had time. Lubang was a small island and American forces would no doubt concentrate on the larger islands. Onado had been specially trained in the art of guerilla warfare, and now he could bring all of his training into actual practice. Onado knew that the only course left for the remaining troops on Lubang was to retreat into the mountainous interior. From here he could wage guerilla warfare on the American troops, harassing them wherever possible, until the day when Japanese forces would return to Lubang.

Lieutenant Onado's orders had been quite clear. His immediate commander Major

Yoshimi Taniguchi of the Special Intelligence Squadron, had written simply, "Officer Onado will proceed to Lubang Island, where he will lead the Lubang Garrison in guerilla warfare." Affixed to the order was the seal of the Eighth Division Commander, Lieutenant General Yokoyama.

Later General Akira Muto, Chief of Staff of the Fourteenth Army, had told Onado, "You are absolutely forbidden to die by your own hand. It may take three years, it may take five, but whatever happens, we'll come back for you. Until then, so long as you have one soldier, you are to continue to lead him. You may have to live on coconuts. If that's the case, live on coconuts."

For Lieutenant Onado, vigorous training in Officers Training School and later with the Special Intelligence Squadron had taught him to obey orders to the letter. There could be no deviation from these orders unless he was directed by a superior officer such as General Yokoyama or Major Taniguchi. Until then Onado would carry on as directed.

On February 21, 1945, an advanced party of fifty American troops landed on Lubang. The next morning the Americans launched a naval bombardment on the town of Tilik. Onado watched in horror as Tilik was completely destroyed. Later from his vantage point Onado could see the main force, the destroyers, and transport ships heading toward Lubang.

Shortly afterward Onado and his men were attacked by American planes and mortar fire. The Americans were aware of their position and Onado knew that retreat into the interior was his only recourse.

The two-month interval between the invasions of Luzon and Lubang had given Onado some time to prepare. He had been able to store rice and ammunition in a central location high in the mountains, and now he and his men began to move in that direction.

For the Japanese soldier, retreat was a difficult concept. Most Japanese soldiers had been taught to fight to the death. To die for the Emperor was more honorable than to retreat. Death was preferable to being captured and Onado's guerilla warfare tactics were contrary to the ordinary soldier's training and outlook on war. Many thus choose to stay and die and despite Onado's commands only some of the men followed him into the interior.

Within three weeks Onado found himself in charge of 150 survivors of the Lubang invasion. He realized quickly that despite all of his efforts food supplies could only last for about two months. Soon squabbling began to break out over the remaining food. Then a large supply of rice was stolen and Onado knew that the only way to survive was to break up into smaller groups which would have to survive as best they could on their own.

As the days passed into weeks, Lieutenant Onado could hear scattered gunfire. Sadly he knew that one of the groups had been discovered by American forces engaged in mopping up activities. With each skirmish he knew that organized Japanese resistance on Lubang was coming to an end and that his small band would have to depend on their own resources and wits.

Onado's small force now consisted of Soichi Shimada and Kimshichi Kozuka. Shimada was an excellent soldier. The only married one of the group, he had a cheerful disposition and was extremely talkative. Shimada came from a farming family and was extremely capable of adapting to life in the jungle. Kozuka was also a good soldier but was the opposite of Shimada. He was very quiet and rarely spoke unless he was spoken to first. Working together the three made an excellent team.

Around the middle of October, 1945, Onado saw the first notice that the war was over. A group of Japanese soldiers attempting to confiscate a cow had stumbled across some islanders who ran when they saw the soldiers. One of them, however, dropped a leaflet that had printed on it in Japanese, "The war ended on August 15. Come down from the mountains."

None of the men believed the words of

the leaflet. Only several days before a group of Japanese survivors had been fired upon by American soldiers. "How could the war be over?" they reasoned.

This was to be the first of many attempts to convince the Japanese survivors that the war was over. In actuality, the Japanese had surrendered on August 15, 1945. On September 2, 1945, General Douglas MacArthur representing the Allied forces, and Foreign Minister Mamoru Shigemitsu representing Japan had signed the surrender agreement. But for Hiroo Onado and many other Japanese soldiers in the South Pacific the war went on.

Toward the end of the year surrender leaflets were dropped from a Boeing B-17. On the leaflets were printed surrender orders from General Yamashita of the Fourteenth Area Army. Once again Onado considered the leaflets to be an enemy trick.

In February, 1946, six months after the end of the war, Onado's group was now joined by Private First Class Yuichi Akatsu. Akatsu was in a weakened condition and proved to be a burden to the other three.

As the months passed more and more leaflets were dropped. Then the men began to hear shouts in Japanese that the war was over. They reasoned that the voices were coming from soldiers who had been captured or surrendered. Onado believed that these soldiers were being forced at gunpoint to say what they did.

The months turned into years and life fell into a pattern for the soldiers. Survival in the jungle became the chief task and slowly the men adapted themselves as best they could to their surroundings. Life was never easy. The jungles of Lubang contained rats, bees, scorpions, centipedes, and snakes as big as a man's thigh. The worst enemy of all were ants, however. The ants seemed to be everywhere and would swarm over anything left unprotected on the ground.

The rainy season lasting from July to mid-October was a difficult period for the men. Often the rain would beat down on them for days at a time soaking them to the bone. The rain would even rot their clothing and caused great discomfort.

But the men survived, despite the conditions, by carefully following a set pattern. Each morning they would brush their teeth with fibers from palm trees and massage their skin with kelp. From time to time they would wash their clothing using lye obtained from ashes as a detergent.

The men were especially careful to take good care of their guns and ammunition for they still considered themselves to be soldiers engaged in warfare. Each day they would clean and polish their rifles. Ammunition was stored in bottles which they confiscated from the islanders.

Food was the biggest problem. Bananas were plentiful on the island and they were the chief staple. Lubang also contained wild buffalos, wild boars, wild chickens, and iguanas which the men shot. But their chief source of meat were the cows which they obtained on periodic raids against the islanders.

Shelter was another concern. During the rainy season the men would build huts constructed from bamboo with roofs made of palm leaves. When it wasn't raining they would sleep in the open on mountain slopes, with bushes or trees for cover.

As leader of the four men, Onado insisted on constant movement so that their position would never become known to the "enemy." Every three to five days they would move to a different location, carrying their supplies with them. It was tedious work but Onado felt that this constant movement was necessary if the four men were to remain an effective fighting force.

Onado's plan was to harass the islanders and Americans wherever possible. In this way he would be carrying out the orders that he had received to carry on guerilla warfare until Japanese forces would return. Imprinted in his mind were the words of his commander.

"It may take three years, it may take five, but whatever happens we'll come back for you."

In September of 1949, four years after the four men had come together Akatsu deserted. He had always been the weakest of the four men and had deserted three times previously. Each time, however, Shimada would go in search of him and the two would return. But this time he was gone for good.

Several months later the three remaining men heard a voice from a loudspeaker shouting that the war was over and to come out. Peering from their jungle hideout, they saw that it was Akatsu leading a small force of six Filipino soldiers. Again they rejected the effort as an enemy trick. They were positive that Akatsu was being forced at gunpoint to lead the enemy soldiers.

In February of 1952, an airplane dropped several packages containing letters from Onado's older brother, telling him that the war was over. The package also contained letters and pictures from Kozuka and Shimada's families. Shimada, the only one of the men who was married, was particularly upset by the photographs which showed his wife and little girl. For several weeks Shimada was in a state of depression.

Then in June of 1953, Shimada was injured badly when he was shot by some Filipino fisherman. His condition gradually deteriorated and he spent the day staring at the picture of his family. Shimada recovered briefly but a little less than a year later he was killed only a half mile from the spot where he had been injured. Onado and Shimada had been together for ten years and for the first time since he had come to Lubang, Onado wept.

But life went on for the two remaining men. Every New Year Onado and Kuzuka would bow in the direction of the Emperor's palace and pledge to be good soldiers during the coming year. Both men were convinced that Japan would never surrender. They had been taught that in training. They believed that Japan would fight to the last man, even if it took 100 years. Little could either man know of the destruction of Nagasaki and Hiroshima by atomic bombs and that the Japanese leaders knew that to continue would be senseless.

The men were aware of some changes however. Early in the 1950's electricity came to Lubang for the first time, and Onado and Kozuka watched as the town of Tilik came alive at night. By this time they had become known as "Mountain Devils" by the islanders who lived in mortal fear of the two Japanese.

In 1959, the largest search party ever was sent from Japan to find the men. Among the party was Onado's brother Toshio. Using a loudspeaker, Toshio began to call out, begging Onado to come out. Onado crept to within 150 yards and could see his brother on a small hill calling to him. For a while Onado couldn't believe his eyes, but then he became convinced that the Americans were using a prisoner who looked and sounded exactly like his brother. Slowly Onado retreated back into the jungle.

In 1965, Onado obtained a transistor radio which he and Kozuka listened to each night. Once again, however, both men thought that the broadcasts were being controlled by the Americans. The men even learned of the 1964 Olympic Games held in Tokyo but reasoned that despite the war both countries had made an agreement whereby the athletes of the world could compete in peace.

It is difficult now to accept some of the reasoning that went into Onado and Kozuka's thinking. But wartime propaganda is very powerful and both men were living in the past. They had been convinced beyond a doubt that the war would go on until Japan was victorious. They had passed the point of being persuaded otherwise.

In October of 1972, Kozuka was shot. Onado and Kozuka had come across some farmers working in the field. As they often did they fired several shots into the air. Usually the farmers would flee leaving behind food and provisions that the two Japanese could use. The trick worked again and Onado and Kozuka were pleased to find a large pot of rice hanging from a tree over a homemade fireplace. Then all of a sudden several shots rang out. Kozuka had been hit. Kozuka stumbled and in a moment several Filipino soldiers came running toward them. Onado fled into the woods cursing in anger and bitterness over the death of his friend. They had walked into a trap.

Three days after the death of Kozuka another search party came looking for Onado. Onado could hear the voice of Chie, his sister, and Tadao, his brother. Then he heard the voices of fellow students from his days in primary school and even the voices of soldiers with whom he had been in training. Again he refused to come out.

On February 16, 1974, Onado went to Wakayama Point where two rivers came together. It had always been an excellent spot to gather good food but on this day Onado noticed something different. He could see a Japanese flag planted on the ground next to mosquito netting which was being used as a tent. Onado approached the tent his rifle ready. Then he saw a man with his head turned facing the river. Onado quickly noticed that the man was unarmed. Then the man turned, stared at Onado, and with a trembling hand saluted. Then he saluted again.

"I'm Japanese. I'm Japanese," said the man. Onado looked around to see if he had walked into a trap but he became convinced that the man was Japanese.

"My name is Suzuki. I've come to look for you. The war is over. Please come back to Japan with me?"

There was something about the young man that appealed to Onado. He had a pleasant manner but Onado wasn't ready to throw away thirty years of work in an instant.

"The war is over," repeated Suzuki. "What do I have to do to convince you? What will make you surrender?"

"Bring me orders," replied Onado. "Bring me orders from Major Taniguchi, my commanding officer, that the war is really over."

Norio Suzuki left Lubang vowing to return as quickly as possible. Suzuki was an adventuresome young man. When he left Japan he had told his friends that he was going to look for Lieutenant Onado, a panda, and the abominable snowman in that order. Some of Suzuki's spirit must have transmitted itself to Onado causing him to listen to the young man.

In Japan, Suzuki managed to find Major Taniguchi and convinced the Major to come back with him to Lubang.

Three weeks later Onado again approached Wakayama Point. Once again he could see from a distance Suzuki's Japanese flag planted next to the mosquito netting. This time a yellow tent was erected next to the netting.

Onado watched until the sun had begun to set. He could see Suzuki walking about. Then, confident that it wasn't a trap, Onado walked toward the flag. Once again Suzuki was standing with his back turned. Upon seeing Onado he turned and shouted. "It's Onado. Major Taniguchi, it's Onado." Suzuki ran toward Onado and embraced him warmly. In a few minutes Major Taniguchi emerged from the tent and stood before Onado. Onado snapped to attention and barked out, "Lieutenant Onado, sir, reporting for orders."

Major Taniguchi seemed unable to believe that it was really Onado who stood in front of him. But then in a loud voice Major Taniguchi read, "Command from Headquarters, Fourteenth Area Army. In accordance with the Imperial Command, the Fourteenth Area Army has ceased activity. Units and individuals are to cease military operations immediately."

Onado stood motionless, unwilling to believe Major Taniguchi's words. But there was no trick. Japan had lost the war and it was all over. Hiroo Onado's private war had ended.

Suddenly the pack which Onado carried seemed to grow very heavy and a wave of relief mixed with disappointment seemed to overcome him. It was all over.

Onado placed his pack on the ground with

the rifle that he had polished every day for thirty years on top of it. Then a new wave overcame him — a wave of anger and bitterness. Thirty years had passed. Onado wondered what he had been doing for all that time. Why had Shimada and Kozuka died? Thirty years of a man's life had suddenly become meaningless and Onado felt a deep sense of depression.

But in the months to come Onado was to realize that his thirty years in the jungle were far from meaningless. In Japan he was received as a war hero. Overnight be became a national celebrity. Accounts of his thirty years on Lubang appeared in newspapers, magazines, and on television.

Hiroo Onado had given the Japanese a national hero. Defeat had deprived Japan of a war hero and Onado's exploits touched the hearts of the Japanese people. There was something about the slightly-built officer that appealed to an entire nation. To the Japanese, Hiroo Onado represented strength, dignity, and integrity. In the end Hiroo Onado felt that he hadn't been defeated; he had won.

Undefeated Predator of the Sea

Shark mania started with *Jaws*, Peter Benchley's powerful book and movie that told the story of a killer shark that created fear and panic along the seacoast of Long Island. The story told of a Great White Shark suddenly turned man-eater that threw the small town of Amity into a state of chaos.

There was something about *Jaws* that appealed to one of humanity's most basic fears — the fear of the unknown. *Jaws* was an intriguing story in the tradition of the great monster stories of all time. The shark lurking in the deep excited a basic fear that has been with us since the beginning of recorded history when early South Sea islanders drew pictures of hated killer sharks on the walls of cave dwellings.

The shark is the last undefeated predator on Earth. The lion, the tiger the alligator, and the grizzly bear have been conquered. But the shark rules supreme in the one area that still is largely unexplored — the sea. As we begin to explore deeper into the oceans of the world we will have to come to grips with a knowledge of the shark. The shark and its habits will have to be studied if we are to harness the resources of the sea. But still there are those who insist that the menace of the shark is more fiction than fact. They say that attacks like those in *Jaws* are practically unknown and there is really little to fear. Let's take a look at a shark in action to see if real fear is warranted.

In his excellent book, *Man-Eating Sharks*, Felix Dennis describes what happened off the coast of South Africa in 1957. It all began on December 18, 1957, when sixteen-year-old Robert Whereley was swimming about fifty yards from the beach near the town of Karridene on the coast of Natal. Suddenly Whereley felt a tremendous pain in his leg. He swam frantically to shore and found that his left leg had been amputated by a shark. Whereley managed to survive the attack.

Two days later, sixty miles to the south, fifteen-year-old Allan Breen was swimming thirty yards from the beach. Suddenly on-lookers were shocked to see Green's arms flailing as he screamed for help. When rescuers reached him he was already dead from multiple cuts and loss of blood.

Three days later on December 23, twenty-three-year-old Vernon Barry was standing in only three feet of water five miles south of Margate Beach. The beach was crowded with swimmers when suddenly Barry was seized by the left leg. By the time the shocked bathers could pull Barry out of the surf he had died from massive blood loss.

Incredibly enough on December 30, fourteen-year-old Julia Painting was standing in almost the same spot where Vernon Barry had lost his life. Once again the shark struck, biting Julia in several places on her body. Amazingly, Julia managed to reach the safety of the beach. Although badly bitten, Julia Painting survived the attack.

By this time a wave of panic and hysteria had gripped the entire area. Many tourists cancelled their vacations and returned home. But as the new year began and no new attacks occurred things returned to normal. Then on January 9, 1958, forty-two-year-old Derryk Prinsloo was peacefully floating in muddy water about ten yards from the beach near the town of Scottsburgh. Suddenly Prinsloo was struck by a shark. Prinsloo had no chance. He died before he could even be brought back to the beach.

Two months passed and once again an ominous calm returned to the South African beaches. Then on April 3, a policeman was attacked and killed while swimming with his brother. Like the other victims there was little that the policeman could do as the shark struck again and again.

Two days later twenty-eight-year-old Fay Bester was standing in four feet of murky water when an immense shark seized her around the waist. Like most of the other victims Mrs. Bester was defenseless. She died before reaching the beach due to shock and massive loss of blood.

In a space of four months seven people were attacked and five lost their lives along a ninety-mile stretch of beach. Obviously the attacks were the work of a single shark, a rogue shark. A rogue shark is often a shark who is either injured or old. As a result such a shark is unable to catch fish in the normal manner. The rogue shark then becomes a man-eater who returns again and again to the same hunting grounds in search of easy prey.

Although such attacks by a rogue shark do occur, they are rare. Far more frequent are isolated attacks by a single shark in varying places. These attacks follow no plan. Indeed, in examining the habits of sharks their unpredictability becomes obvious. A shark cannot be catalogued in the way many animals can and anyone dealing with a shark can never be sure of how a shark will react in a given situation. At any rate the shark is an awesome creature. Let's follow a shark as it prepares for an attack. This will give some indication of just what mankind is faced with in dealing with a shark.

First of all a shark swimming in the open sea is a beautiful but deadly sight. A shark's body is a remarkable product of millions of years of evolution. A shark's body has no bones but is composed almost entirely of cartilage. This makes the body highly maneuverable as it moves through the water. The shark must move continually. It never sleeps but is constantly in motion, searching for food. Since the shark is heavier than water this constant motion is necessary to prevent the fish from sinking to the bottom of the ocean.

In an attack the shark utilizes every one of its remarkable senses in zeroing in on its target. First the shark calls upon its amazing sense of smell. At 500 feet a shark can detect one part of blood in 100,000,000 parts of ocean water. This makes any bleeding creature in instant danger of a shark attack.

Now the shark will begin its famous weaving pattern in approaching the target. As the shark picks up the scent in one nostril, it automatically turns in that direction. Then as the signal gets stronger in the other nostril it turns to that side, creating the weaving pattern that is so frightening.

As the shark gets closer its sense of hearing becomes acute. At 1,000 feet a shark can pick up the vibrations of a struggling fish or human. As it moves closer and closer its sense of hearing is even more acute.

At 200 feet the shark's sense of touch is utilized. A shark has a longitudinal canal system that runs the length of its body just below the skin. These canals are filled with sensor cells that can detect minute changes in pressure. In this way a shark is able to "feel" objects hundreds of yards away.

At fifty yards the shark's eyesight is used. A shark, although color-blind, can easily differentiate between an object and its background. This difference is enhanced if the object is moving.

The shark will then circle its prey several times before moving in for the kill. Although it is the most dangerous predator in the sea, the shark does have its natural enemies and is cautious before it attacks. Then, opening its powerful jaws, a shark will strike. Recently, scientists using a device called a "Snodgrass Dynomometer" were amazed to learn that an eight-foot-long shark has a biting power of 3½ tons per square centimeter. Imagine the power of a Great White Shark which is often twenty, thirty, and even close to forty feet long.

A shark's teeth are another wonder of the animal kingdom. A shark has several rows of teeth. As one tooth is lost another will move up from the next row to take its place. This continuing process occurs throughout the life of the shark. Each tooth is also like a triangular knife and with the force of the powerful jaws it is no wonder that an amazing list of objects has been found in a shark's stomach.

In *Man-Eating Sharks*, Felix Dennis lists a few of the objects found in a shark's stomach. These are: a good leather wallet, a two-pound coil of copper wire, a goat, a turtle, a raincoat, three overcoats, a car license plate, grass, tin cans, the skeleton of a cow, leggings, buttons, leather belts, shoes, the propellor of an outboard motor, six hens, a rooster, twenty-five quarts of water, three bottles of beer, a reindeer, a blue penguin, part of an oak tree, a handbag, a powderpuff, and a wristwatch.

Many of these unusual objects are devoured in the shark's famous feeding frenzy. In a feeding frenzy hundreds and even thousands of sharks are attracted to a specific area. The sharks, then in a mad frenzy to obtain food, will swallow anything in sight. In a feeding frenzy nothing is safe. Sharks have been known to devour small boats and virtually anything — even each other — in this frenzy. One thirty-foot Great White was found with a fifteen-foot tiger shark which it had downed in one gigantic swallow.

In a shark, then, humans are faced with as deadly a creature as can be found. The Great White is the most deadly of the species. These usually stick to the deepest parts of the oceans although occasionally they come close to land.

The Tiger Shark is another deadly species. It gets its name from the dark brown stripes that are found on the sides of young Tiger Sharks. Tiger Sharks can grow to between eighteen and twenty feet in length.

The Bull Shark or Whaler Shark is characterized by a blunt round snout. It is famous for "bumping" its victims before the attack. Bull Sharks are also known for swimming up rivers leading to the sea. Bull Sharks have been known to swim down the St. Lawrence River and have even caused problems in Lake Michigan.

The Mako is an excellent game fish highly sought after by fishermen. Renowned for their great strength, a Mako is also extremely dangerous.

Other types of dangerous sharks are the Porbeagle, the White Tip Shark, and the Hammerhead.

What can be done about the menace of the shark? Many things have been tried. All types of poisons have been tried without success. Although some poisons will kill a shark, the time factor would be of no help to the average bather who couldn't be expected to carry poisons into the water with him.

During World War II the U.S. Navy developed various shark repellents. These repellents were all designed to confuse the shark's senses in one way or another. Most of the repellents contained a dye which would color the surrounding water, supposedly making the intended victim almost impossible for the shark to see. Other repellents contained various irritants designed to discourage an attacking shark. All of these proved almost useless.

More recently the U.S. Navy developed an apparatus called a Shark Screen. A Shark Screen is really nothing more than a large plastic bag with three inflatable rings around the top. The person in the water then crawls into the bag where he can float with some degree of safety. Once inside the bag the shark cannot see or smell the person. In addition, if the person is bleeding the blood does not spread into the surrounding water. In actual tests sharks have tended to ignore persons in such bags unless they accidentally bumped into them in which case the bag will tear. In addition, the bag is of little use to the average bather who can't be expected to carry a plastic bag to the beach with him.

Several years ago an Australian named Frank Arpin came up with a method that seemed foolproof at the time. The method, known as the Bubble Barrier, was simple but seemed to work. Arpin placed a large hose punctured with tiny holes in the water. By forcing air into the hose a wall of bubbles was formed. At first sharks were reluctant to cross the wall of bubbles, but once they grew used to the bubbles they crossed as if nothing were there.

The most effective method of all has proved to be one of the simplest and one of the oldest. This method is the wire mesh fence which can be placed in the water protecting an entire beach or swimming area. Even when holes occur in the mesh, sharks are reluctant to enter the area. No doubt this is due to their natural reluctance to become trapped. Only two known shark attacks have ever occurred in beaches protected by wire mesh.

But despite their success, wire mesh fences are extremely costly. In addition they offer no protection in the open sea. Today scientists have found that since sharks are attracted to certain sounds and vibrations they can also be repelled by some frequencies and pitches. But researchers are worried that such methods can do damage to the brains of sharks. As a result more research must be done in this area.

In many cases common sense is an effective deterrent. The scuba diver swimming with a string of bleeding fish is inviting disaster. The bather who swims alone, far from shore, in water where shark attacks have occurred is certainly inviting disaster. Swimming at night, when sharks are often feeding should also be avoided.

Although the shark has been known to kill and maim humans, the possibilities of an attack are still extremely remote. Actually more people are killed by bee stings and lightning each year than by shark attacks. There is as much danger of being killed driving to the beach as there is from shark attacks.

Then, too, the shark is doing its job in the natural order of the animal kingdom. The shark provides an extremely valuable service for mankind. It is a scavenger which has been called the "garbage collector of the sea" and its huge appetite helps rid the oceans of dead fish and other unwanted objects.

Humans will have to learn to live with the shark. It was here long before we came and may be here long after we leave. The shark is a deadly creature but still there is a certain beauty about it as it moves through the water, performing the tasks for which it was intended.

The Lost Tribe

Men have dreamed of going back into time to witness great events of the past. Science fiction stories have been written telling of machines that can suddenly transport a voyager backward to the year of his choosing.

In 1971, on the Island of Midanao in the Philippine Islands, history came alive when a group of natives was discovered living in the tropical rain forest in the exact manner that early cave dwellers must have lived. The small tribe known as the Tasaday Indians may be the last of their kind living on Earth. Their existence provides us with invaluable clues as to what early people were like. The Tasadays may be the most incredible people on Earth, living in a state that in some ways is more advanced than our own highly technological society.

The Tasadays were first discovered in 1966 by a hunter and trapper named Dufal, a member of the Manubo Blit tribe. The Manubo Blits are one of many tribes that exist on Mindanao, the southernmost island of the Philippine archipelago. It is sparsely populated and covered with mountains and volcanoes, some of which are still active. Mindanao is very close to the equator and as a result densely wooded rain forests cover the island.

Dufal discovered the Tasadays quite by accident on one of his long journeys in search of food for his tribe. He came across the small band in some of the most rugged terrain in all of southern Mindanao. The Tasadays lived in a valley between two rugged mountain chains. Trees, many of which were 200 feet tall, provided a natural barrier. All of this, together with the natural jungle vegetation and the absence of any trails, makes the region almost impenetrable from the outside.

Dufal managed to communicate with the Tasadays by using a combination of sign language and a few words that both understood. In the following years Dufal became friendly with the Tasadays who referred to him as "he who walks through the forest like wind." Dufal was amazed at the simplicity of the tribe and tried to help them by introducing the bow and arrow to them. Dufal also taught the Tasadays to trap. Both innovations were the first advances by the Tasadays in thousands of years.

In 1971, Dufal contacted Manuel Elizalde, Jr., chief of the Philippine government's Presidential Arm for National Minorities. Dufal knew Elizalde and his group, shortened to Panamin, to be friends of the natives of Mindanao. Elizalde and Panamin hoped to protect the natives against land grabbers, mining companies, and foresters who sometimes took advantage of the simplicity of the natives. Dufal arranged for a meeting between the Tasadays and Elizalde.

In 1971, Manuel Elizalde, other government officials, and anthropologists arrived by helicopter and met the Tasadays. What they saw amazed them. Clothed only in thin loin cloths or grass skirts, the tribe was huddled together in these natural caves in the side of the mountain. Elizalde was amazed to find a tribe more primitive than any he had ever seen in his experiences with the natives of Mindanao. Elizalde was positive that no other group in such primitive conditions could exist anywhere in the world.

At first Elizalde found the Tasadays to be very timid, but as time passed he learned that they were a friendly and kind people.

The tribe numbered only twenty-four people. There were ten men and five women. Of the nine children, only two were female. Elizalde learned that once married, the Tasadays remained faithful to each other for life. Such an arrangement was not usual among primitive people, and Elizalde realized sadly that with only five married couples, the future of the tribe could be in jeopardy.

As time passed Elizalde learned some amazing things about the tribe. The tribe had no words in their language for war or hate. Crime was unknown. No one ever struck another person and parents never spanked their children. In general they were a warm and affectionate people and Elizalde realized that the Tasadays were more advanced in many ways than any people he had ever met.

But existence in the tropical rain forest was never easy for the tribe. Until the introduction of the bow and arrow the Tasadays had no tools except for a crude axe. The axe was made of stone and had a handle of wood. They were tied together by rattan vines. The axe was similar to the crude axes made by early cave people found in other parts of the world. The axe had no value as a weapon but was used only to break open hard fruits or stems.

The Tasadays also made fire in the same way as early cavepeople. A slender wooden rod was placed in a wooden socket which was then moved rapidly back and forth by the palms. After about ten minutes this would produce a spark which would then ignite threads of dried vegetable fiber.

Traveling in the rain forest was almost impossible for Elizalde and his group but for the Tasadays it was relatively simple. They jumped easily from rock to rock or from log to log. Also the Tasadays, especially the younger children, were adept at swinging from vines hanging from the trees.

In this manner they gathered their food. Their diet consisted of tadpoles, frogs, crabs, and fish gathered from the streams. They also ate the pith from palm leaves as well as flowers, berries, and wild bananas. Until Dufal had introduced hunting and trapping the Tasadays had never eaten meat, but now they learned to cook over an open fire and even to smoke their meat in order to preserve it.

But in most ways the Tasadays remained incredibly simple. They had no knowledge that they were a part of the Philippine Islands. They had never seen the sea and had no word for this in their vocabulary. They did know of the existence of two other tribes, the Sandukas and the Tasanfanor, but didn't know if they were still in existence.

The Tasadays had no knowledge of numbers or counting. They had no concept of time and no one in the tribe knew how old he was. They had no metal tools other than those introduced by Dufal. They had no domesticated animals, nor any idea of agriculture. They had no pottery, but instead used bamboo sections as containers. Elizalde realized also that the Tasadays may be the only people on the face of the earth who have not discovered how to use tobacco or had some form of smoking.

The Tasadays depend on cooperation and the family structure for their survival. Each family is an independent organization that may adopt orphans or even widows or widowers. Competition does not exist among families. Axes, bows and arrows, and other objects may be used by anyone on a cooperative basis. There is no leader of the tribe nor is there any division of labor. Each person does what he is best suited for. When there is an extreme shortage of food, the children of the various families are fed first.

Elizalde and the anthropologists realized then that they had discovered a most unique group of people. Although completely lacking in natural possessions, the Tasadays had attributes that far outstripped material objects. The anthropologists could point to the absence of war, hatred, anger, and greed. The family structure was stronger than any that they had ever encountered and the sense of cooperation and love among the tribe was unequaled.

For the Philippine government the discovery of the Tasadays presented some complex problems. Should the Tasadays be introduced gradually to a more modern way of life? Already Dufal had introduced several objects which had made life easier for the tribe. What problems would these innovations cause? Older members of the tribe remembered a time when animals such as deer were their friends and could be touched and petted. Now they withdrew upon sighting the Tasadays.

There was little time to waste. Already logging companies had begun building roads into the deepest parts of southern Mindanao. The survival of the primitive existence of the Tasadays was only a matter of time.

With the cooperation of President Ferdinand Marcos of the Philippines it was decided to set aside a 50,000 acre preserve for the Tasadays. The reserve would be off limits to all but a very few.

It was decided to make every possible effort to preserve the Tasadays as they had been found. Anthropologists could then study the tiny band, hoping to learn as much as they could about their ways.

The Tasadays present a unique opportunity for modern people. With our problems of pollution, crime, poverty, war, and greed, we have changed almost completely from the way that we might have been at one time. The Tasadays can provide us with a living microcosm of our past. Perhaps we can learn and profit from the simple lives of this lost tribe.